Orville Bright

Graded instruction in English for the use of teachers

Orville Bright

Graded instruction in English for the use of teachers

ISBN/EAN: 9783337124656

Printed in Europe, USA, Canada, Australia, Japan

Cover: Foto ©Paul-Georg Meister /pixelio.de

More available books at **www.hansebooks.com**

GRADED INSTRUCTION

IN ENGLISH

FOR THE USE OF TEACHERS

Orville T. Bright

Entered according to act of Congress, in the year 1881, by C. M. Bright, in the office of the Librarian of Congress, at Washington.

THE OSHKOSH TIMES

PREFACE.

The object in preparing this course of instruction in English was solely for use in the school of which the author is principal. The solicitation of fellow workers in Chicago who have watched its success, is the reason for publishing it in its present form.

Many teachers, perhaps the majority, will disapprove the plan; but it has already many friends. There is no denying the fact that the teaching of good English, as shown by the results, is a sad failure. As common a charge as any brought against the public schools by the journals is that pupils leave the grammar schools without being able to write a decent letter. The worst of it is that the charge is true as concerns the majority of the schools, and it is just as true that such results are unnecessary.

The teacher who attempts the following plan without understanding the whole scope and intent of it, at least to include her own grade, and who does not make daily preparation for the lesson to be presented, can have only partial success—or failure.

What is wanted with little children is *practice* and not *reasons.*

This cannot be too strongly impressed. Hence in the early language lessons, leave out the "*why*" altogether.

A large majority of all ungrammatical expressions may be grouped under a limited number of topics. It is believed that these topics may be successfully presented to children in primary grades. This is the special object of this course of study.

For the suggestions that led to the preparation and adoption of this syllabus, the author is indebted to a visit to the public schools of Aurora, Ill., and to the kind courtesy of the superintendent, Mr. Powell.

DOUGLAS SCHOOL, CHICAGO, Sept. 1, 1881.

GENERAL REMARKS.

In giving language lessons to little children, the prime object should be to lead the children to talk freely about the objects and incidents that come within their observation, and through means of this freedom to lead them to use correct forms of speech. If a thought is correctly expressed in oral language it will be in written, provided the child can spell correctly. Hence the prime importance of what is so greatly neglected—teaching children to talk correctly.

To be sure, there are many outside influences, especially the practices of the home, that will operate against the success of the teacher. But it must be remembered that while in recitation the mind of the child is on the alert for impressions, and that the word of the successful teacher is "law and gospel" to the learner. Hence an hour a day spent on this subject by an earnest teacher will largely, if not entirely, overcome the influences referred to.

It will rarely be necessary to give points of instruction out of hand. They may all be drawn from the children by skillful questioning, and nothing pleases the child more than to furnish the correct form of speech. It will be found very rare indeed that any error will be made that none of the children will be able to correct. All that is wanted with little children is the correction with no attempt at reason therefor.

While any incorrect form of speech in school should be corrected at any time, still if dependence for learning and habitually using correct language be placed upon these corrections only, failure will be the result as it has been heretofore. The impression one is able to make in the face of all opposing influences will not be a permanent one, unless there be a controlling idea in the mind of the teacher when conducting a language exercise, so that the questions and answers shall be brought to bear upon the particular construction or constructions to be impressed.

By taking up one topic of instruction at a time, and in natural order, by constant reiteration in the sentences of the children, of the correct construction wanted, by the correction of errors which will present themselves in these same sentences, and by means of these corrections, placing in contrast the incorrect and the correct forms of speech, impressions will be made upon the minds of the children that nothing can efface, and not even the home influence can overcome.

By securing the freedom of speech, before alluded to, the incorrect expressions used upon the play ground and in the homes of the children, will be brought before the class for their criticism and correction, and it will not be long ere the same errors will be noted when not made in the schoolroom.

In all cases of incorrect expressions, be sure that they are heard without repetition by the teacher. This will lead children to criticise each other. Any pupil who makes a correction should do so clearly and distinctly, and by means of emphasis bring the incorrect and the correct form into strong contrast. One of the greatest benefits to be derived from the recitation will be gained by giving exact regard to this instruction. For instance this sentence is heard: "There is three apples on the table." The hands are raised for correction. James said, "There *is* three etc." for or instead of "There *are* three etc." After a little practice the correction may be, "He ought to have said etc," each word being spoken distinctly. At other times the correction may be made as follows: "James ought not to have said etc." Thus "had ought" and "hadn't ought" will be banished.

There is no study in which an efficient teacher can awaken greater enthusiasm than in English, and there certainly is none of greater importance. The almost total neglect accorded to it in primary schools is very strange, to say the least.

Present one topic at a time, and thoroughly, before going on to another. Recollect again, there is to be no technical instruction with little children, no reasons for the use of words as employed. The use of technical terms may be taken up when it is easier to do with than without them. Secure correct *use* of words and sentences through correct *practice*.

The plan advocated will appear more fully in the following topics for instruction, which have been divided into eight grades or years, as this term may be taken as the average time required in preparation for high school studies. This classification may be easily adapted to any graded school.

FIRST GRADE.

1.

The use of *a* and *an*.

The teacher presents objects or their names, and the children us a or an as they repeat each name. Make the exercise rapid, working with the pupils both individually and in concert.

2.

The use of nouns in the singular and plural, combining them with the correct forms of verbs in sentences, and the use of this and that with their plurals.

The teacher uses the terms "one" and "more than one."

Whenever practicable, require all answers to be complete sentences.

Let the children name the objects in the school room, one and more than one, as they shall be designated.

Follow this exercise with a prepared list of familiar names, the teacher naming one and the children more than one.

Then the teacher names the plural and the children the singular. Then the teacher gives one form and the children the opposite.

To secure the correct form of the verb, first use the objects at hand, requiring something to be told or asked about each in the singular and then in the plural, or vice versa.

The teacher holds to view a book, and secures the sentences: The book is old. The book has leaves, etc. By presenting more than one: The books are old. The books have leaves, etc.

After using the objects at hand take the list of words as before, requiring each to be used in a sentence, always following the use of one form of the noun with the other.

Secure the use of two or more nouns with one verb, or one noun with two ore more verbs, thus leading the children to condense their statements in description.

Especial attention will be required in sentences beginning with *there*, in changing from one to more than one. These difficulties only add to the zest of children.

This and *that* with their plurals, will be used from the beginning.

Showing a pencil, What is this?

That is a pencil.

That pencil is in your hand.

Showing two, the plural forms are obtained.

The child takes the pencil or pencils, and the use of this and these are obtained. First use with visible objects, then without.

The points already indicated, taken in connection with the natural timidity of children on entering school, will furnish the basis for 'instruction for a long time.

The teacher must not try to crowd too much into the first few weeks or months. Her main object should be to secure freedom of expression on the part of the pupils.

3.

Use of adjectives.

The special object is to facilitate expression of the apparent qualities of common objects, and thus lead slowly to the description of such objects. Require complete sentences each expressing one quality of the object presented. Then two or more qualities in one statement or question, being careful about the repetition of *and*. Thus:

The pencil is long.

The pencil is long and round.

The pencil is long, round and sharp.

Farther on an excellent practice will be to require a reason for some of the statements made. Thus:

I think the chair is old because, etc.

I know the sponge is wet because, etc.

4.

Use of adverbs.

The errors appear in using adverbs derived from qualifying adjectives. The teacher performs some action and the children tell how it is done; or the action may be performed by one of the children. For instance, the teacher walks slowly across the floor.

What am I doing? You are walking.

How am I walking? You are walking *slow*, will be the answer of nine-tenths or more.

Always get the correct answer from the children, and have it repeated in concert. Then folllow with:

What *kind* of walking is this? That is *slow* walking.

How am I walking? You are walking *slowly*.

Bring out in the strongest possible manner, the contrast in the correct use of the adjective and of the adverb derived from it.

Get from the children as many words as possible describing the same action, and the use of more than one of these words in the same sentence.

Give thorough drill in the use of words describing actions that can be seen by the children. Afterwards any other actions may be described, or the words may be given for use in the sentences, alternating adjectives and adverbs. It must be borne in mind that the number of adverbs of manner given in this grade must be quite limited, and only those in most common use.

5.

Use of the personal pronouns as the subjects of verbs, both singly and in combination with nouns or with each other.

Secure facility in changing from one to more than one, or vice versa, when used singly in sentences. This, as all other exercises in language in this grade, should be begun with objects visible to the children.

Next have the pronoun combined with one noun. For instance:

Who is standing? I am standing.
Who else is standing? Mary is standing.

Say the two answers together. A variety of answers will follow. Me and Mary, Mary and me, I and Mary, Mary and I are standing. Secure the correct use of each pronoun, first with a single noun, then with more than one noun, then use one pronoun with another, etc.

Give especial attention to the use of the verb *was* with pronouns requiring the verb *were*.

Nobody says we is, you is, or they is; but we was, you was, and they was, are exceedingly common, especially, you was.

The thorough handling of this topic will require great skill and patience, especially with children of foreign parentage.

6.

The question will arise as to the spelling of the words used. This should be acquired as rapidly as practicable. Of course, little or nothing can be accomplished in this regard at first, but after a few months, or during the last half of the grade the words used by the children should be spelled both orally and by writing in sentences.

7.

Thorough drill upon the correct use and orthography of the following words, taking the most common ones first:

be	bee	right	write	
dear	deer	read	red	
eye	I	son	sun	
hear	here	their	there	
hour	our	to	too	two
know	no	wood	would	
knows	nose	which	whose	
knot	not	wrote	ought	
meat	meet			

8.

Teach the children to avoid the use of *real* for *very*, (This error is almost universal.) of *have got* for *have*, of *aint* and *shant*, of *lots of* or a *lot of*.

The manner of making corrections alluded to in the general remarks, will entirely avoid the use of an auxiliary verb with *ought* in statements. Practice the same in questions.

9.

Oral repetition of little stories, told or read by the teacher, or one of the children; or of stories or incidents that have come to the children's knowledge outside of school. Also oral description of objects in the school room, or that may be presented to the children. In short, any means that an intelligent teacher can use to make the children feel at home in school, and induce them to talk freely. The object is not only to secure freedom in the expression of ideas, but also in correct expression.

10.

The foregoing comprise the topics of the grade for oral exercises. Having a good basis on which to build, the written work will be rapidly accomplished. This will consist of writing sentences similar to those already used, with correct use of period and interrogation mark, capitals to begin sentences and proper names, and the word I. Each pupil should be able to write his own name, residence, the name of the school, of his teacher, and of the principal.

All writing of sentences should be neatly done. Whenever practicable, any sentences written in a careless or slovenly manner should be copied before they are inspected by the teacher.

The writing of sentences except from copy should not be undertaken during the first two-thirds or three-fourths of the grade. Writing is not to be expected in Topic 8.

The work indicated will demand *time* each day. A daily exercise of ten, fifteen or twenty minutes for sixty or seventy pupils will not answer. From forty-five to sixty minutes, divided into such exercises as will best suit the teacher's purpose, may be very profitably devoted to this subject, and that without detriment to any other; provided, of course, that the pupils are so classified that the same lesson may be given to all in the same room, and that they attend school all day.

SECOND GRADE.

1.

If the second grade work is begun at the begining of the school year, review briefly the first grade topics.

In reviewing the use of *this* and *that*, give thorough drill on the use of these words with *sort* and *kind*. These kind of flowers. Those sort of apples, are expressions in almost universal use.

2.

The use of different forms of the irregular verbs. No part of the English Language is more fruitful in errors than the use of these verbs, and their correct use in school will be something entirely new to very many children.

The following lesson is indicated merely as suggestive to the teacher.

Such verbs should be chosen for the first lessons, as will present something for the children to see in the recitation. Take the verb *break* for example. The teacher holds to view a stick of convenient length.

If I want to make two pieces of this stick, what shall I do? Break it.

Require this and all other answers to be complete sentences. Let the sentence be repeated several times, and *break* be spelled singly and in concert.

The teacher breaks the stick.

What did I do? Broke it.

Tell me so. You broke the stick.

Spelling as before.

The teacher holds the two pieces to view.

What have I done with this stick? Broke it.

Tell me so. You have broke that stick.

That does not sound right.

Hands will be raised for correction, and the right word will be given in the sentence.

All repeat the sentence together, spelling as before.

The pupils repeat break, broke, broken, very distinctly after the teacher, and spell the words again.

Then obtain a variety of answers to each of these or similiar questions.

How many ever broke anything, and when?

How many have ever broken anything?

What had I done to this stick when I showed two pieces? and other questions, securing the answers has broken, is broken, was broken, etc., each in a complete sentence.

The teacher may now call rapidly for each form in sentences given by the children, all being ready to correct errors, which will be numerous.

This will be sufficient for a half hour's lesson.

Present other words in similar manner each day, reviewing words previously given, until all the verbs in the list can be used with precision. Require every form of every verb to be spelled when given, so long as there is any doubt about its being spelled correctly.

Topic 4, in first grade, may be greatly extended in this connection by simply asking "how?" when the sentences are given. As:

Use some form of *eat* with yesterday.

I ate my dinner yesterday.

How?

I ate my dinner slowly yesterday.

Any special words called for in the sentence should be spelled.

By requiring a different adverb with each succeeding verb given in a recitation, or many different adverbs with the same verb, the vocabulary of the children will be extended and their facility of expression greatly increased.

As the children get used to the recitation and to the requirements of the teacher, the questions may be very brief, simply to suggest the idea to the child.

When we consider the comparatively small number of the irregular verbs, and the fact that they are used many times more that all the others combined, he importance of thoroughness in this topic cannot be overstated.

Appended is a list of verbs to be presented. The teacher will choose the verbs as she wishes to present them:

break	do	hang	ride	sing
bite	drive	hide	rise	sleep
bring	eat	hold	run	speak
begin	fly	hurt	ring	slide
blow	forget	hear	stand	steal
buy	feed	keep	shake	take
come	freeze	know	see	tear
catch	fall	leave	strike	think
choose	find	lose	say	throw
cut	give	lie(recline	sit	teach
drink	go	make	sell	write
draw	grow	read	send	wear.

The above list will require long and patient drill extending, may be, over many weeks.

3.

Correct use of the nominative form of the personal pronouns after *is*, *was* and *were*.

A child stands, and the teacher asks:

Who is standing?

I am standing. (*I* given with emphasis.)

Who is it that is standing?

It is me that is standing, will be the probable answer.

The following sentences will be obtained by a little tact and skillful questioning in regard to actions observed;

It is I that am standing.

It is he that is standing.
It is he and I that are lifting the chair.
It is she that is walking.
It is we that are reciting.
It was they that were whispering.
It is you who are hearing our lesson.
It was you who were writing on the board, etc.

Have the correct manner of giving the sentences repeated many times, singly and in concert, to impress the unusual sound upon the minds of the children. Vary the sentences to use the verbs mentioned both in questions and in statements.

4.

The almost inevitable use of the noun in the possessive singular, in the sentences of the children, renders it necessary that they should early learn to write it correctly.

Without giving any rule, call for the spelling of such expressions as, John's hat, the boy's book, etc., depending simply on the practice to produce the result. Then require the same expressions to be written on the slates.

Use only singular nouns in connection with the names of the objects possessed.

5.

Use and orthography of the following words in addition to a thorough review of those in Topic 7, in first grade:

| aunt ant | stair stare |
| ate eight | steal steel |

bare bear	grate great
blew blue	knew new
brake break	lain lane
buy by	lead led
coarse course	made maid
fore four	pair pare pear
flour flower	pail pale
ring wring	pain pane
road rode rowed	pray prey
rose rows	tail tale
sail sale	threw through
sea see	whole hole
sent cent	won one
some sum	ware wear

The use of these words together with those in first grade, should form a part of the exercises throughout the entire time in the grade. Children will be especially interested in discriminating in their use, and a variety of interesting ways to present them will occur to any intelligent teacher. One or two only will be mentioned. They may be printed or written, one on each of as many cards as there are words, so plainly as to be easily seen by all the pupils.

Then, as the teacher presents the cards, the children in turn form sentences containing the words seen. The teacher can thus remain quiet and the children do the talking.

The teacher may speak one word, and the pupil use all of that sound in one sentence. Then spell the words in order of use, etc.

These exercises never fail to rouse the enthusiasm of little children.

6.

Use of adjectives in the comparative and superlative degrees.

Two sticks of unequal length are given to two children who stand before the class.

Who can see any difference in the sticks?

One is longer than the other.

Which stick has James?

James has the longest stick, will be the answer. By repeating the former question and securing emphasis upon the word longer, the correct answer, James has the longer stick, will be obtained.

Follow this with the opposite quality.

Then present three or more sticks and the pupils will soon see the distinction in the use of the comparative and superlative.

Two pupils of unequal height will secure the use of taller and shorter, heavier and lighter, etc.

Two books, the words longer and shorter, wider and narrower, cleaner and dirtier, etc.

The attention of children is easily held in this exercise as they must in every case observe the qualities which they express.

7.

Pronunciation of words.

The children should tell readily the number of syllables in a word, and know the meaning of the teacher when she says a certain syllable is accented. Aside from practice in reading and in other lessons, lists of words may be placed on the board and the children pronounce them, enunciating very distinctly, after the teacher.

Then they may pronounce in the same manner when the words are pointed out, and following this, individual pupils may do the same. Two or three minute exercises, two or three times a day, on lists of ten words well selected, will be of the greatest benefit.

8.

In addition to Topic 8 of first grade, teach the avoidance of *learn* for *teach*, of *plenty* for *plentiful*, of *don't* for *doesn't*, (few people make this discrimination) of *off of*, *off from*, or *onto*, of *as lives* for *as lief*, of *good ways* or *long ways* for *long way*.

9.

In addition to what is required in Topic 10 in first grade, the children should be able to write the situation of the school, the names of the streets in the vicinity, any given date, as July 15, 1880, the names of days and months with their abbreviations, and such contractions and abbreviations as occur in the reader.

10.

The time given to English in this grade should be about one hour a day under the same conditions as mentioned for first grade. Since the children, if properly taught, can write readily on entering the grade, the time should be about equally divided between oral and written exercises.

The use of capitals extended from first grade only to include names of days and months.

In punctuation add the use of the comma in a series of words, and to follow a name denoting address.

The sentences required in writing will involve points of instruction presented in this and the preceding grade.

The work of the first grade may be all thoroughly reviewed and kept fresh in the minds of the children by constantly combining in the sentences required different points of first grade topics. In fact, this should be done all through the course, and it may be without at all impairing the force of the instruction in hand.

11.

In order to promote connected expression of thought, extend Topic 9, of first grade, adding oral description of pictures. If facilities are ever furnished for the intelligent teaching of reading, means will be at hand to greatly aid in developing this topic. But earnest teachers will invent means. Suppose an exercise in sight reading. Let each pupil face his classmates, read a portion of some interesting story or description, then close the book and give an outline of what he has read, or of the story from the beginning. The intelligence and and clearness in expression of children who have been well trained in such exercises would be a revelation to the ordinary hum-drum teacher. Such exercises are impossible with readers which the children know by heart.

The feasibility of carrying this topic into writing in second grade is very doubtful.

THIRD GRADE.

1.

Without making any parade about it, begin the use of the terms noun, common, proper, singular. plural and possessive, *without definitions.* It is easier to use them than not, and the children will soon become familiar with, and use them correctly.

2.

Rapidly review Topic 2 of second grade and add the use of the following verbs.

bind	kneel	shoot	swim
bleed	hit	show	swing
build	lay	shrink	tell.
burst	lead	sink	weep
dig	meet	slay	wet
lend	pay	spring	win
feel	send	stay	wind
fight	set	stick	wing
forsake	shine	string	
grind	shoe	swear	

Each word spelled.

3.

Correct use of adjectives after the verbs, look, seem, appear, feel, taste and smell.

The country looks beautiful—not beautifully. The apple tastes delicious—not deliciously. The rose smells sweet—not sweetly. I feel bad—not badly—(if *bad* can be used for *ill*.)

The parents will question the correctness of the teacher's instruction in this topic, and the inevitable question is, "Doesn't pleasantly tell *how* it looks?" By a judicious selection of other adjectives the expression will be easily shown to be correct.

4.

Correct use of different forms of *who*. Who did you see? Who did you go with? are used fifty times oftener than the correct expression.

Make the practice as great as possible until the use of each word is thoroughly understood, but do not write incorrect sentences upon the board—certainly do not allow them to remain there.

Each word spelled.

5.

Use of *who* to refer to persons, of *which* to refer to things, and of *that* to refer to persons and things.

Indicate the correct use through questions and answers, as:

Shall I say the man which went away has returned?

The dog whom I saw is lame?

The horse who is at the door? etc.

The answers should show that either of two words may be used.

6.

As preparatory to the use of the dictionary, the distinction between vowels and consonants should be taught, that is, the pupils should be able to tell which letters are vowels and which consonants, omitting words containing w and y.

They should be able to give the long and the short sounds of vowels, and distinguish these sounds when pronounced in words.

7.

Add to Topic 7 in first grade and Topic 5 in second grade, the use and orthography of the following words:

ail ale	presence presents
aught ought	pride pried
bald bawled	pries prize
ball bawl	prince prints
berry bury	rain rein reign
bough bow	rap wrap
choir quire	seen scene
fair fare	scent sent cent
forth fourth	sees seize seas
gait gate	sense cents
groan grown	sell cell
hall haul	stake steak
hair hare	throne thrown
heal heel	told tolled
him hymn	wade weighed
idle idol	wait weight
need knead	way weigh
pain pane	weak week
peace piece	wrote rote
praise prays	.

8.

Same as Topic 7 of second grade, applying Topic 6 of this grade.

9.

Teach the children to avoid the use of *less* for *fewer*.

I have less apples than you.

Of *expect* for *suspect*. I expect he has left the city—(expect a past event!)

Of *banister* for *balluster*, of *quantity* for *number*. We saw a great quantity of birds.

Of *anybody else's* for *anybody's else*, of *stopping* for *staying*. Our friends have been stopping at the hotel two weeks.

Also review similar topics in preceding grades.

10.

Rule for the possessive singular and plural of nouns and application of the same. Teach the rule in three parts, as follows:

The possessive of singular nouns is formed by adding the apostrophe and s.

The possessive of plural nouns ending in s is formed by adding the apostrophe.

The possessive of plural nouns not ending in s is formed by adding the apostrophe and s.

The learning of the rule will amount to nothing without a very great amount of practice. That it can be understood and applied by the children usually found in third grade has been demonstrated.

11.

Thoroughly review the more difficult topics of second grade.

12.

Topic 11 of second grade extended.

The stories, incidents and descriptions to be produced in writing as well as orally. The written productions should be very brief at first.

The teacher should pass around among the children directing, commending and criticizing. Several of the compositions may be read by the children. For the greater part this work will of necessity be upon the slates, which can receive only the general attention of the teacher. Occasionally, perhaps once a week, the compositions may be written upon paper and the errors marked by the teacher. These papers when returned should be re-written and the errors noted and avoided. The best ones may be read to the school. Care must be exercised here, however, not to discourage the poor writers.

13.

Letter writing may be and should be taught to children at a very early age. Begin the subject in this grade, but do not try to overdo the matter. A little child's letter is of course a very simple affair, but it may be correct in form, and the sentences correctly arranged.

As an incentive allow each to send the first commendable letter to father or mother through the mail, with some commendation of the teacher.

The time devoted to the subject in this grade should be about the same as in the second. It will depend somewhat upon the course of study.

FOURTH GRADE.

1.

In addition to the grammatical terms used in Topic 1 of third grade, use the terms *verb, pronoun, present, past, future,* and *perfect* as applied to verbs, it being understood that *perfect* has reference to the use of have, has or had with the verb.

None of the terms are to be defined. Their use will be more convenient and the children will soon become familiar with them.

2.

A limited use of quotation marks, omitting divided or broken quotations.

This will necessitate the further use of the comma. Add the use of the exclamation point.

4.

Rules for the use of capital letters.

5.

Rules for forming the plural of nouns.

The regular plural of nouns is formed by adding s or es.

Special rules for plural of nouns ending in y, o and f or fe. Also writing the possessive singular and plural of these nouns.

6.

After the foregoing topics have been presented, the topics of the first and second grades should be reviewed so far as there is necessity to make them perfectly familiar.

Each topic of third grade should be taken up carefully and many of them extended. In Topic 6, include w and y, and distinguish in their use.

Special attention to Topic 10.

7.

Same as Topic 8 of third grade, adding the use of the dictionary.

Be sure that the children can find words and tell their pronunciation as well as orthography and definition. To this end there should be general exercises in finding words and explanations from the teacher and pupils as to determining the pronunciation. The marks denoting the long and the short sounds of vowels should be learned. Reference to the bottom of the page will suffice for the others, as they do with grown people. Quickness in finding words should be cultivated and commended.

8.

In addition to reviewing similar words in preceding grades, teach the use and orthography of the following:

air heir	might mite
aisle isle	oar ore o'er
altar alter	passed past
all awl	quarts quartz
aloud allowed	read reed
beau bow	scull skull
bell belle	sew so sow
been bin	seam seem
better bettor	shone shown
bread bred	side sighed

dense dents	sighs size
dew due	slay sleigh
false faults	sole soul
fir fur	tacks tax
flea flee	toe tow
grater greater	vain vane vein
heard herd	yale veil vail
higher hire	waist waste
leaf lief	way weigh
lie lye	

9.

Composition and letter writing upon the same plan is suggested in third grade, only more extended. The suggestions in Topic 11 of second grade, should be followed and extended.

Topic recitation may be introduced in this grade, but this must be done in such way as to prevent the committing and reciting of passages from the text book—that is so far as it appertains to language exercises. These same recitations may be written as compositions.

Also easy subjects may be assigned, discussed and written upon under an outline which the teacher places upon the board.

10.

The use of the terms *subject* and *predicate* in very simple sentences and dividing the sentences into the same, as:

The horse—is walking.

An old man—sits on the piazza.

Declarative or interrogative sentences not more difficult than the above.

11.

Teach correct plural of such words as spoonful, pailful, etc., use of *in* and *into* with verbs indicating motion.

Avoid using *balance* for *remainder*, of *some* for *somewhat*, of *funny* for *queer* or *strange*, of *cute*, and the double abomination *real cute*.

Review similar topics.

12.

An examination in this grade may include any topic thus far given. This is true of any grade and need not be repeated.

FIFTH GRADE.

1.

Definitions of subject and predicate. Distinction between general or modified subject and predicate and simple or unmodified subject and predicate.

2.

Analysis of sentences within the following limits: The sentences to be simple, declarative or interrogative, with no transposition from the regular order in the arrangement of elements.

The analysis shall consist of classifying the sentence, naming the general subject and predicate, and the simple subject and predicate.

3.

Definitions of noun, common and proper noun, person, number and gender, and of each class of the last three.

Without definition of case the pupils shall designate the nominative, the possessive, and the objective case of nouns, and give reasons therefor. The nouns in the nominative case to be confined to the subject of the finite verb, in the possessive case to exclude apposition, and the objective case to immediately follow its governing word. No rules to be given. Confine this topic to sentences analyzed.

4.

Definition of adjective No classification. Compare without definition of comparison, and tell to what noun the adjective belongs. Exclude adjectives belonging to pronouns and predicate adjectives.

Confine the work to the sentences analyzed.

5.

Definition of verb. Name principal parts. Classify into regular and irregular, transitive and intransitive, avoiding verbs in the passive voice. Confine the verbs given in sentences for parsing to the indicative mode, then each of the six tenses may be designated, but not defined.

Agreement of the verb with subject in person and number.

6.

Without definition name the more common prepositions as they occur in sentences analyzed, and tell the relation shown.

7.

Definition of pronoun. Parsing personal pronoun

within the limits of the parsing of nouns. Declension of personal pronouns. Exclude definition of declension and exclude the word *thou*.

8.

Use of dictionary and pronunciation of lists of words as in previous grades.

Use of the terms root, prefix and suffix. Application of the same in words having English roots, as in the word dishonestly. What is the root? The prefix? The suffix? Nothing more.

9.

In addition to review of similar words in previous grades, present the following:

assistance assistants	guessed guest
attendance attendants	hew hue
base bass	hoard horde
beach beech	hoes hose
board bored	hoop whoop
brews bruise	in inn
brows browse	lessen lesson
cellar seller	levee levy
chance chants	links lynx
chews choose	loan lone
colonel kernel	mail male
core corps	miner minor
creak creek	mussed must
cue queue	nay neigh
currant current	night knight
dam damn	paced paste
dependence dependents	pedal peddle
earn urn	plain plane

c'er cre	pore pour
ewe yew you	residence residents
fellow felloe	right rite write wright
fisher fissure	roar rower
flew flue	soar sore sower sewer
gamble gambol	soled sold
gap gape	tense tents
grease Greece	tide tied
grocer grosser	

10.

Composition writing as in fourth grade. In addition to the writing in school the pupils may occasionally choose a subject and write upon it at home.

A subject with topics for writing in school should be assigned several days before the time for writing, and the children encouraged to investigate and think about it. Purely impromptu composition is not desirable. Descriptions of imaginary journeys, and biographical sketches to a limited extent, will be very profitable.

11.

Letter writing. An excellent practice will be to tell the children two or three days beforehand that the next letter will be written from New York, Paris or some other interesting place. They will seek information in regard to the same, and thus two ends will be served.

They should also be instructed as to writing letters of application for business situations, or answers to advertisements in regard to the same.

·12.

There should be an hour set apart as often as once each week for the reading of compositions and selections, and for recitations. Selections for reading or recitation should never be presented without the previous approval of the teacher. See note at the end of the course.

13.

The various topics of the previous grades must be kept in review.

SIXTH GRADE.

1.

Elementary sounds, classification into vocals, sub-vocals and aspirates. Analysis of simple words into elementary sounds and classification of the sounds with reasons.

Definitions of terms used.

2.

Letters. Classification into vowels and consonants. Make clear distinction between elementary sounds and their classification and letters and their classification. Diphthong and triphthong. Definitions and illustrations of terms used.

3.

Words. Classification as to syllables, simple and compound, primitive and derivative.

Definitions of root, prefix and suffix. Practice upon forming derivative from primative words with definitions of both primitive and derivative words to show the changes in meaning. Also ask for definitions of short lists of words formed from the same foreign root, as dispose, suppose, propose, etc. It will not be profitable in this class of words to pay any attention to the meanings of the different parts, as the meaning of the word itself will very likely not conform to the meaning of the parts.

Definitions of all terms used.

4.

Classification of words into parts of speech. Definition of part of speech, and of each class.

5.

The noun, excluding nouns in apposition, nominative independent, nominative absolute, and nominative by pleonasm. The predicate nominative to be confined to the verb *be.*

Parsing to be confined to sentences analyzed.

6.

Pronoun. Same limitation as for nouns. Confine the work to personal pronouns. Definition of declension. Agreement with antecedent.

7.

Adjectives, classified into limiting and qualifying. No classification of limiting adjectives. Definition and manner of comparison. Use of the adjective with the verb to form the predicate and parsing of the same.

Parsing confined to sentences analyzed.

8.

Verb. Confine work to tenses in the indicative and potential modes.

Classification according to form and meaning.

Principal parts, voice, modes used, tense.

Definition of all terms used.

Apply in sentences analyzed.

9.

Adverb. Classification, comparison and use in sentences analyzed.

10.

Prepositions in common use.

11.

Conjunctions. And, but, or and nor. Let them be known as co-ordinate conjunctions. Their office in sentences analyzed.

12.

Interjections—to name them is sufficient. No rules are to be required in parsing.

13.

Analysis and synthesis of simple sentences. Analysis to consist of classifying the sentence, naming subject and specifying its word and phrase modifyers; same of predicate.

The phrases to be classified as adjective or adverbial. Only prepositional phrases to be used. Omit imperative sentences.

14.

Correction of errors in construction, with reasons for those indicated in the primary grades.

15.

Use of dictionary and pronunciation of lists of words as in 5th grade.

16.

In addition to similar words in the preceding grades, present the following:

ascent assent	innocence innocents
bad bade	lade laid
beer bier	lacks lax
berth birth	leak leek
candid candied	mantel mantle
ceiling sealing	medal meddle
cite sight site	meer mere
coat cote	mews muse
council counsel	might mite
crews cruise	moat mote
crewel cruel	ode owed
cymbal symbol	paired pared
Dane deign	peal peel
die dye	plough plow
dire dyer	principal principle
done dun	rice, rise (noun)
dost dust	rung wrung
draft draught	rye wry
dyeing dying	seer sere
ewes use yews	stationary stationery
feat feet	soot suit
fined find	tare tear
foul fowl	throes throws
franc frank	vary very
frays phase	vial vile viol phial

gilt guilt	vice vise
gored gourd	holy wholly.
hail hale	

17.

Same as Topics 10, 11 and 12 of fifth grade. Add the writing of promissory note, and ordinary receipt for money.

18.

Previous topics to be kept in review.

SEVENTH GRADE.

1.

Synthesis, analysis and parsing of sentences. No definite limit can be assigned for the sentences, but their difficulty may be governed by the fact that there is to be another year's study in the same subject.

Learn and apply the rules of construction both in parsing and correcting false syntax.

Rapid syntactical parsing, and study of the meaning of constructions.

2.

Same as Topic 17, of sixth grade, adding the writing and answering of notes of invitation.

3.

Review similar words before presented and add the following:

abbe abbey	main mane Maine
bail bale	maize maze
bark barque	marshal martial

barren baron
barreness baroness
bay bey
bolder bowlder
breach breech
cannon canon
canvas canvass
cast caste
cede seed
ceil seal
chased chaste
chord cord
clause claws
coward cowered
cousin cozen
cypress cyprus
deviser devisor divisor
doe dough
ferrule ferule
fort forte
gild guild
kill kiln
knave nave naive
liar lyre

marten martin
mean mien
meat meet mete
metal mettle
mold mould
peer pier
pole poll
reek wreak
rest wrest
roe row
rough ruff
rout route
sailer sailor
sane seine
serf surf
tacked tact
taper tapir
team teem
tear tier
tide tied
tire Tyre
wain wane
waive wave

4.

Pronounciation of lists of common words which are frequently or usually mispronounced. By the aid of a little handbook, prepared for the purpose, this exercise may be made very interesting without special labor on the part of the teacher. It will be a great incentive to individual investigation.

EIGHTH GRADE.

1.

Synthesis, analysis and parsing of all constructions. Any of the selections of the reader should be analyzed, both as to grammatical construction and the meaning of the author. Of course, one cannot be *well* done without the other.

In analysis the recitation should not be too minute. Classifying the sentence, naming the subject and predicate, and classifying their word, phrase, or clause modifiers is sufficient, unless some peculiar or obscure construction occur in one of the elements.

In parsing, require only the words about which there may be difficulty.

Do not dwell upon matters with which the pupils are familiar.

Any false syntax to be corrected with reasons.

2.

Use and orthography of the following words:

adds adz	levee levy
adherence adherents	load lode
allegation alligation	manner manor
auger augur	palate pallet
auricle oracle	peak peek pique
bight bite	pearl purl
borough burrow	plait plate
censer censor	pleas please
cere sear seer	plum plumb
cereal serial	. port Porte
cession session	radical radicle

choler collar	raise rays raze
complement compliment	real reel
cygnet signet	reck wreck
days daze	rheum room
demean demesne	rigger rigor
exercise exorcise	shear sheer
fain fane feign	seignior senior
faint feint	serge surge
fate fete	sleight slight
filter philter	stile style
freeze frieze	stoop stoup
hart heart	subtler suttler
impassable impassible	succor sucker
indict indite	suite sweet
invade inveighed	thyme time

3.

Same as Topic 2 of seventh grade.

Upon any subject with which the pupil is familiar, he should be able to write intelligently and correctly. He should be able to write letters correct in form and expression, to write notes of introduction or invitation, and to answer the same, and to write correctly any ordinary business form. This is not too much as a test of written work, and the pupil who cannot, in eighth grade, do the work indicated should be exceptionally stupid—at any rate so far as the English language is concerned.

4.

Same as Topic 4 of seventh grade.

5.

The whole subject to be reviewed and completed so far as grammar school work can do it.

NOTES.

A. As a means of cultivating easy use of language, there is nothing that excels a well conducted recitation. Whenever practicable, recitations should be topical, and during the recitation of his topic a pupil should not be interfered with. Question and criticism will come in their proper place, and should come freely from the pupils.

The ability to recite upon any given topic for one, two or three minutes, in well chosen language, is invaluable.

In order that topic recitations may be well conducted thorough preparation is necessary on the part of the teachers. This is one reason why they are not adopted. The indolence of teachers leads them to prefer to sit behind text book like machines, read questions, and look for answers.

This disgraceful method, or want of it, is still common even in what are called good schools. In its use the children are not thrown upon their own resources for the use of language, but answer in monosyllables or in little phrases learned, verbatim from the text-book.

B. The selections for reading or recitation in general exercises, should be only such as have been approved by the teacher. The tendency with the children is to look for something humorous. The taste may be easily controlled and gradually led to seek such selections as will elevate and strengthen the character.

This will require literary research on the part of the teacher than which nothing, certainly, can be of greater benefit.

In the primary grades, the committing of single stanzas containing especially beautiful thoughts, or of short selections for concert recitation, is a most excellent practice. A store of such selections should be gathered so that something may be called for every day.

C. General exercises, as to frequency and arrangement, must be regulated for the wants of each school. They should be dignified in character and carefully arranged so that the children will respect as well as enjoy them. Do not allow them to become tiresome through too great length, either as a whole or as to parts. The recitation, in a clear voice, of a short sentiment by each pupil of the class, makes a pleasant feature of such exercises.

An hour each week, for which careful preparation has been made, given to essays, readings, recitations, sentiments, and singing, will be the pleasantest hour of the week to both pupils and teachers.

D. When a child can read fluently and intelligently at sight, the teacher's work with him as to *how* he shall read may be considered pretty well done.

It is not at all necessary for the school teacher to try to fit him for public reading nor for the stage.

The question as to *what* the child shall read is one

of the greatest importance, and strange to say, one that receives but very little attention, in school or out of it.

The reasons that parents do not guide and control in this matter arise from various causes, ignorance, want of interest, want of time (imaginary but potent), and want of literary training or taste.

To be sure no outline of study calls for attention to this subject from the teacher, but it is one of such interest and importance that no true teacher after once having thought seriously of the matter, can shirk its responsibilities.

The minds of the children crave food, almost as universally as do their bodies.

If left to themselves they will seek that which excites their emotions only, but which will be as unhealthy mental stimulus as would be a diet of sweetmeats for the body.

This subject should receive the earnest attention of certainly all teachers of grammar grades.

Let each teacher study and think about it. Make lists of books and periodicals which can be conscientiously recommended to the children to read. The parents in general will be very glad of such assistance, and in many cases will cheerfully procure the books recommended.

Of course there are many standard books which may be recommended on their reputation, but let there be no mistake about any book in the list.

Perhaps no more valuable plan than that lately so successfully tried and adopted in the Wells School of Boston, can be devised. Copies of the same book are obtained from the public library for all the pupils in a class. On a given evening instead of the regular school lessons all are expected to read a certain portion of the book. The next day it is discussed in school and forms a most interesting literary exercise. As a language exercise it beneficial effects are remarkable. Unfortunately the facilities afforded in Boston are peculiar to that city, but perhaps the plan may be approximated in some way through the ingenuity of skillful teachers.

Keeping a record of books read will stimulate and control the habit of reading. The mere idea of reporting to their teacher will often deter pupils from reading trashy books. In condeming any book the child should be made to understand the reason of its hurtfulness.

One plan is to have a blank book in which each pupil shall have a space for himself, divided for each month. At the end of the month ask for a written list of books read by each pupil together with the names of the authors. These may be recorded in the book referred to by one of the pupils. The teacher should look over the list and commend or condemn the reading matter. As often as once each quarter the result of each pupil's reading may be announced.

In this way much lasting good may be accomplished. The dangerous classes in the community are not the readers.

A teacher's aim should be to study, not how little work and responsibility the letter of the law demands, but how she can be of the greatest benefit to the children under her charge, both as to their improvement while there, and also as to the formation of habits which will promote the happiness and usefulness of their whole lives.

www.ingramcontent.com/pod-product-compliance
Lightning Source LLC
Chambersburg PA
CBHW030723110426
42739CB00030B/1352